THIS IS JAMES SILVERTH hopefully be many. What st his slowly receding hairline tips to help those going thr

James' inspiration con... ..... novels. These range from superhero stories to self-help books. Two of his favourite authors and cartoonists are Gene Luen Yang and Adrian Tomine who combine humour and heart in compelling narratives to keep the reader engaged. Their illustrations are some that James has used to practice, and improve, his own drawing ability.

His professional career has always been design focused. He is currently working as a CAD Technician which involves a lot of technical drawing and working to specific detail. This book has been a way for James to flex his creative mind and produce something that can continually help others.

A Brief Guide *to* Going Bald

James Silverthorne

SilverWood

Published in 2023 by SilverWood Books

SilverWood Books Ltd
14 Small Street, Bristol, BS1 1DE, United Kingdom
www.silverwoodbooks.co.uk

ISBN 978-1-80042-244-5 (paperback)

British Library Cataloguing in Publication Data
A CIP catalogue record for this book is
available from the British Library

Page design and typesetting by SilverWood Books

**The information contained within this book is strictly
for educational purposes. If you wish to apply ideas contained
in this book, you are taking full responsibility for your actions.**

A BRIEF GUIDE TO GOING BALD

50 Tips to Help You Bald with Grace (hopefully)

Introduction

I am a man with a follically-challenged cranium. I have now, unless I want to undergo high-cost surgery, come to accept that fact and I am happy.

Growing up I was convinced that I would be blessed with long luscious locks forever; that my hair would work in any style and that maybe one day I would get randomly scouted for a shampoo advert. What I failed to realise at that early stage in life was that my dad and maternal uncle were both bald and my paternal uncle was heading the same way. Despite many an effort to maintain the hair I had; the time came for me to admit defeat.

Going bald is a fear that many people have. The thought of losing our hair is one that fills us with dread. Our looks are defined by our particular hair style. We gain more confidence knowing that our hair looks good, and there is so much emphasis on the need to have hair that, it can be overwhelming. Some can go through life and not care what the latest trend is, whilst others try to keep track of what it will be for the year.

This short book is for those who are having trouble with the transition of losing their hair and how, once you have taken the plunge, it can actually make you feel better. My hope is that it somewhat comforts and supports those people, even if only in a small way.

The Receding Begins

Starting with a positive: the receding is not anything to worry about. It's a process that often takes a very long time and you can have many good hairstyles with a slightly less prominent front line.

When you notice that the hair is taking slightly longer to grow back, that's when there's a problem. The common thing to look for with a receding hairline is the formation of an 'M' shape.

1 The Receding Begins

The Gradual Shortening

Upon noticing that your hair isn't quite as full as it used to be, you may find yourself gradually getting it cut shorter and shorter. For example, if you're a male, going for a grade 3 cut, which, before you know it, becomes a grade 2. Styling of some sort can still be done and at the time will feel like a good idea. However, when you look back upon it, you will perhaps question your decision.

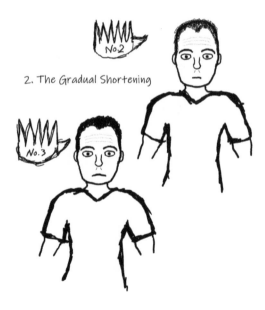

2. The Gradual Shortening

Worrying About Your Looks

Worrying about how and what you look like is a struggle a lot of people go through at an early age. We try to keep up with the latest fashion, trends and celebrity styles.

When you get to this stage of balding, this worry will become even more prominent. If you are one of the lucky ones who do not particularly care what people think, then you'll be okay. But for those who become more self-conscious, try not to let it get you down. There is more to who you are than your hair.

3. Worrying about your looks

Checking Your Hair Every Ten Minutes

You'll probably reach a point in the hair loss process where you feel the need to constantly check your hair, especially if you are still trying to style it. You'll leave the house happy with how you look, but a short while later, the panic will kick in. If it's raining, you'll want to check. If it's windy, you'll want to check. Even if it's sunny, you'll want to check. Once you get this feeling, it's hard to focus on anything else.

4. Checking your hair every 10 minutes

Using Thickening Shampoo

There are products available on the market that promise growth and thickening when you use them. I think these are more of a placebo than anything else but can certainly build up your confidence. I myself went through a stage of trying out a certain brand. To this day I don't know whether it helped or not.

5. Using thickening shampoo

Trying to Cover With Elaborate Techniques

You may find yourself looking for a variety of different ways to cover or hide the baldness. This could be by dying your hair, or trying more elaborate hair styles like cutting the sides to a much shorter length than the top. These techniques may work for a little while but ultimately just delay the inevitable.

6. Trying to cover with elaborate techniques

Cursing the Genes You've Inherited

I should've known I was going to go bald. Just by looking at my family members it was quite obvious. No matter how much I thought I could avoid it, the reality was, I was never going to have a full head of hair when I got older. If you have relatives who are bald, the chances are that you may end up that way too and, like me, will blame your mum and dad for the bad genes they have passed down.

7. Cursing the genes you've inherited

Being Envious of Your Friends

It can be hard to take when you're going through the process and all of your friends still have a full head of hair and luscious locks that they constantly style. It can certainly knock your confidence and even make you feel less attractive. You'll stare at photos and hate how it's only you. Don't let these feelings grow; it's just your mind playing tricks on you. You still have many desirable qualities that people gravitate towards.

8. Being envious of your friends

Trying to Work Out the Science of Why It Happened to You and Not Your Siblings

If you have siblings, younger or older, who do not appear to be having the problems you are having, you'll find yourself asking, "Why me and not them?". This doesn't just stop with the hair; it can be many other things too, like height or brains or athletic ability. It may feel slightly unfair, as if they have all the good genes, but this isn't true. You never know, they could be looking at you and thinking the same thing. Plus, as mentioned previously, if it's common in your family, they may end up going the same way eventually.

9. Trying to work out the science of why it happened to you and not your siblings

Your First Grade 1 Cut

This feels like a scary step to take, and that first cut may feel horrible. However, if you've been slowly getting shorter with the grades anyway, you have probably been thinking about this for a while and are at the point now where a grade 2 looks silly and a grade 1 is a necessity. Once you have done it, going back to trying to grow it longer feels rather strange and you'll relish when you have to cut it again.

10. Your first grade 1 cut

Losing a Few Inches Off Your Height

Like high heels, your hair style can give you a few extra inches of height. The styles that involve hair products to defy gravity will make you feel taller than you are. When you no longer have the ability to do this, you'll discover how tall you really are, and I hate to say this, but it will be smaller than you'd hoped. Don't worry though, because being tall or short doesn't change who you are as a person.

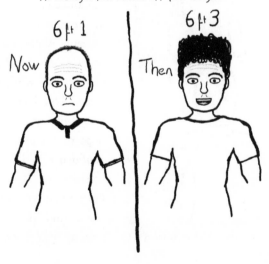

11. Losing a few inches off your height

The Consideration of Treatments

There are many treatments that can be used to help with hair loss. They can work really well but do come with a price tag. You'll find yourself googling what is involved a countless number of times, and you'll have numerous back-and-forths with yourself on whether to get it done. There are surgical procedures such as transplants, and there are those more short-term but effective options, like hair systems.

Of course, there are always wigs as well. They are an option that can be mocked if they don't look right, and you may think of the cheap, wire-like Halloween ones when wigs are suggested. But there are amazing shops out there that specialise in affordable, stylish and realistic hair pieces. The choice is yours. Whichever you choose, I hope that it gives you the confidence and happiness you deserve. If not, then I'm hoping by reading on you'll find the tips you need to make it easier.

12. The consideration of treatments

Cutting Your Hair Becomes a Weekly Thing

When your hair starts to thin, you'll notice that the back and the sides can still be pretty thick and prominent, but the top is the complete opposite. You will then start to realise more and more that thinning hair looks a lot better the shorter it is. You will find that if you leave it a certain amount of time, it just starts to look silly. Other people may not see it, but you will. Where previously it could be a while before a haircut, you'll now find it's at least a weekly thing.

13. Cutting your hair becomes a weekly thing

Telling Yourself You Can Still Grow Hair
If You Really Want To

If you take the plunge into cutting off all your hair while it can still somewhat grow, you'll constantly tell yourself that if you were to leave it for a few weeks, it will grow back as full and thick as it used to. Unfortunately, this is not true, and it will probably look slightly patchy. I speak from experience and, believe me, it's not worth it anyway.

14. Telling yourself you can still grow hair if you really want to

Your First Grade 0

This stage is even more daunting than the grade 1 cut. Just the thought of having to remove the attachment from your shaver can cause panic. However, by now, you are more than likely at the stage where the back and sides are growing slowly, and the top is pretty much non-existent. Remember the feeling you had after the grade 1 cut? After going for a grade 0, you'll feel even better.

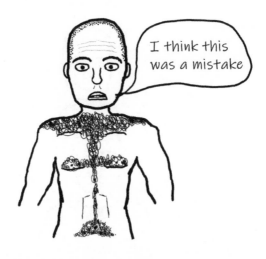

15. Your first grade 0

The Fear That All Bald People Look the Same

Like when you get a new car, you suddenly start to see that make and model everywhere. When you go bald you'll notice more and more bald people.

Now, this may not be the case for all, but a recurring thought I had when I saw a fellow baldy, was, "Do I look like that? That must be what I look like." For peace of mind, you do not look like every other bald person you see; it's just not possible.

16. The fear that all bald people look the same

The Battle of Beard or No Beard

One decision that is hard, and will continue to be, is whether to have a beard or be clean shaven. You'll grow a beard, then after a few months decide it looks wild and untamed, so you'll shave it off. Upon shaving it off, at first, you'll think: this was a great idea – I look so much younger!

After keeping it up for a few weeks you'll decide it doesn't look right and it takes some effort to shave constantly, and thus, will grow it again. It's a vicious circle. I'm always doing it because I just can't make up my mind. You may be more decisive than I am. My advice would be do what makes you feel good and don't let others determine your decision.

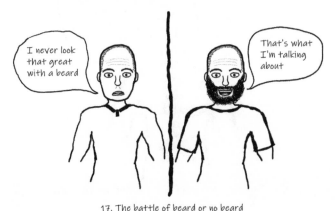

17. The battle of beard or no beard

Cursing Your Hair for Continuing to Grow
Everywhere Else But On Top

I was once told that you don't lose the volume of hair on your
body. Meaning that, once you lose it on top, it will grow
everywhere else. Personally, I have found this to be true. My neck
and shoulders are becoming much worse. You may like how it
looks and let it grow. Or, like me, you could decide it's a bit much,
and that, when it does get too long, it makes you feel like a yeti. I
will add, keeping it neat and tidy does take time. The decision is
yours but, either way, you'll complain to yourself and question
your body an awful lot.

18. Cursing your hair for continuing to grow
everywhere else but on top

Wearing a Hat is No Longer a Fashion Statement – it's a Necessity

A hat is a simple but amazing invention. What was once used as an accessory to make you feel cool and trendy, is now an absolute must, especially in those extreme weather conditions. In summer your head will get burnt and it's not a nice feeling (showering becomes a painful experience). In the winter your head will get cold. Whether it's a beanie or a cap, just make sure that you are prepared.

19. Wearing a hat is no longer a fashion statement - it's a necessity

Your First Clean Shave

This is the big one. Grade 0 is no longer doing the job, the peach fuzz look isn't working, and it's time for the clean shave. If you were nervous about the other two, then crank that up by 10 because this is a whole new level. If you decide to use the razor blade method, both the feel of putting shaving foam everywhere, not just on your chin, and the sensation of the blade on your scalp will be really strange, and may slightly freak you out. If you decide to use an electric razor, it's not like how you'd cut your hair with clippers, so be careful.

Be very slow and cautious with both methods. It's not easy the first few times. Do stick with it though because it does get easier, and it's definitely worth it.

20. Your first clean shave

Needing a Variety of Mirrors

The more mirrors you have the easier it is. One mirror is not enough. This may seem silly to say, but believe it. Yes, okay, you can just wing it and hope for the best, but why? This could result in a missed patch of hair which will look stupid or, slightly more serious, a cut on your head. You may find it awkward to hold a mirror in one hand and shave your head with the other, but it's more sensible and ultimately quicker when you can see what you're doing.

21. Needing a variety of mirrors

Comparing Yourself to Celebrities

One thing that you may find yourself doing is googling bald men, specifically bald celebrities. Now, when you do this, you will discover that most bald famous people look good and, when you look at yourself, you don't quite feel that you do. This may lead to experimentation, but, I can say with confidence, this negative attitude towards yourself is all in your head and most people will tell you it actually suits you.

22. Comparing yourself to celebrities

People Will Feel the Need to Touch Your Head

For some reason a shaved head to people is like a light to moths. People will be drawn to it. I'm not sure what the fascination is, but there will be an increase in hand to head contact. Some will be nice and ask if they can touch it. Others, the less considerate, will just take it upon themselves to either stroke, pat or rub your head. If it gets too much, be firm and speak up. Don't let it continue if you feel uncomfortable.

23. People will feel the need to touch your head

The Constant Jokes

You're now an easy target. People will make jokes. All. Of. The. Time. You'll need to be quite thick-skinned, and if you can, make fun of yourself before someone else does it. There's the old saying, "If you don't laugh, you'll cry". Make sure it's the laughing that you are doing as already touched upon; it obviously means you're an outstanding individual in all other areas.

24. The constant jokes

Using Shampoo No Longer Makes Sense
But You Do It Anyway

It's common knowledge that shampoo is used to clean your hair. Certain brands claim to give more volume, others can help with dandruff. When you shave your hair off, it may seem like buying and using shampoo is slightly pointless. However, for me, there's something not quite right about using shower gel or body wash on your head. If you are in the beard phase, you'll need shampoo for that anyway. There are 2-in-1 or 3-in-1 options, which if you're shopping on a budget, can be a very good purchase.

25. Using shampoo no longer makes sense but you do it anyway

Photo 1

I would do my hair before going out and think it looked okay. But once the weather had its say, it most certainly wasn't. I do believe this was a time when I was using thickening shampoo as well.

Photo 2

Looking at this now, I can't believe I ventured into the outside world. The comb over is not a good look. I should have definitely shaved it off at this point.

Photo 3

Another wonderful hair style that I thought was really working. I would let the top grow and constantly trim the sides. It probably didn't help that I was doing it myself.

Photo 4

This was a period when I was experimenting with different styles. The one in question was a skin fade. It didn't quite work because the hair on top was thinner than the sides even with them cut.

Being Asked If You Ever Had Hair

When you meet new people, they are only going to ever know you as being bald. This can be quite frustrating. You may find yourself having to answer such questions as: "Did you ever have hair?" Or, "Was that a choice?" Or, "Do you like being bald?" The important thing to remember is that most people are just curious and are not saying it out of malice.

26. Being asked if you ever had hair

Being Told By People They Can't Imagine You With Hair

Following on from being asked if you ever had hair, you may find people say phrases like, "I can't imagine you with hair". I think this is meant as a compliment. At least, that's how I take it. But at the same time, it can strike a nerve and cause you to think thoughts like: I looked good with hair. I'll prove them wrong.

27. Being told by people they can't imagine you with hair

That was when it was very long

That looks so weird! See it doesn't look right seeing you with hair

Waiting For Your Friends to Go Bald Too
Because You Want Them to Know How It Feels

Point number 8 was feeling envious towards your friends with hair. Now, there will come a time when they themselves (at least some of them) will start going through the receding and balding process. It's important to be sensitive and try to offer them advice. The likelihood is, they will not take the advice and instead try to figure out what's best for themselves, which you, of course, respect. Show them support nonetheless. However, at the same time, don't be afraid to occasionally make a joke at their expense, not to be mean, but because you know how it feels. Again, make it something they can laugh about, rather than hide.

28. Waiting for your friends to go bald too because you want them to know how it feels

The Feeling of Putting Shaving Foam On Your Head Will Always Feel Strange

Shaving foam caters for both the mature and immature. It's perfect to use for pranks on family and friends but, of course, its main purpose is to help when shaving. When putting it on your face or legs, it feels relatively normal and is quick to get used to. When putting it on your head, however, it will feel very strange. This sensation is multiplied when using the razor. I'm not sure you ever entirely get over this feeling.

29. The feeling of putting shaving foam on your head will ALWAYS feel strange

It Gets Harder To Take Off A T-Shirt

Something that does become quite annoying and slightly more difficult is putting on and taking off clothes that go over your head. This is because your lovely, freshly-shaven cranium will now feel like Velcro that T-shirts and jumpers will stick to. You will need to use a more methodical method of getting dressed and undressed and come up with a new technique that, admittedly, you'll probably forget when you're in a hurry. Just make sure that in certain situations (wink, wink, nudge nudge) you factor it in. If you don't, it may kill the mood.

30. It gets harder to take off a t-shirt

Getting Fluff Stuck To Your Head

Another problem which can become very annoying is how easily your head becomes a haven for fluff. What makes this worse is that it will go unnoticed. You can be going about your day when suddenly a friend will say, "Oh, you've got something on your head". This is very nice of whoever said it. However, the concern for you is how long it's been there.

31. Getting fluff stuck to your head

Save Money on Hair Products

There is a financial silver lining that comes with going bald. You no longer have to spend loads of money on hair products. From small things like hair gel, hairspray, shampoo and conditioner, to the electrical items like hair dryers and straighteners. It all adds up for those with hair but for you, you no longer have that burden and can proudly walk past that aisle next time you're in a supermarket.

32. Save money on hair products

But Razor Blades Do Cost Quite a Bit

Okay, so this point slightly contradicts the last. Although you'll be saving money on a lot of hair products and electrical appliances, razor blades do come at a price. The razor itself is normally pretty cheap, unless you want a 10 blade, flexible head, glides to the contours of your face one, but the blades can really set you back depending on the brand.

You may find another method that is easier for you, in which case your hard-earned dollar is safe. I have tried a few of these and personally, I find that disposable razors work fine and are a cheap alternative.

33. But razor blades do cost quite a bit

Spend Less Time Getting Ready to Go Out

Do you remember a time when you spent so long trying to get your hair looking perfect? All those precious minutes wasted because there was one strand of hair out of place?

Well, that will no longer be a problem. Going out becomes a less arduous task and gives you the upper hand on those you are getting ready with, if they are not bald as well. Although, try not to waste that time choosing which clothes to wear instead.

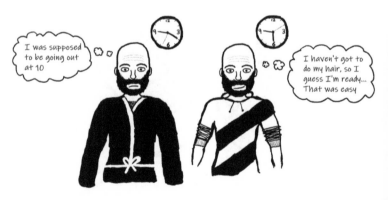

34. Spend less time getting ready to go out

35

Spend More Time in the Bathroom

Again, we have another two points here that may seem to contradict each other. Although you will find yourself spending less time getting ready, when you need to cut your hair, you'll find that you spend an awful lot more time in the bathroom. This is because of how frequently you'll feel like you need to cut your hair. You may find it easier to make it part of your morning routine, or perhaps make it an evening ritual. Either way, it's a lot more time.

35. Spend more time in the bathroom

Wake Up Looking as Good As You Did When You Went to Sleep

I'm sure you have heard of 'bed head'. Luckily for you, this is not a saying you'll ever have to use again. You will wake up looking as good as you did when you went to sleep, apart from maybe a few bags under your eyes. While others will have to doll themselves up, you can continue your day knowing you are all good.

36. Wake up looking as good as
you did when you went to sleep

The Weather Has No Effect

For those with hair, every venture into the great outdoors is a battle with the elements. Every gust of wind, rain drop, and sweat caused by the sun is a cause for panic. As highlighted in point number 4, this will be something you've experienced and know well. Now, however, that will no longer be a problem. The weather will not influence your style anymore and gone is that itching that you need to check your hair. You can walk down the road with confidence knowing that you still look good and, if you want to, can giggle at those having a bad hair day.

37. The weather has no effect

A Clean Shave is Now a Must

After your first clean shave, you may have had quite a mix of emotions: happiness because it actually looks good; sadness because there's no going back now that it's been done; worry because it's not easy to do, and you don't want your head to look like Freddie Kruger's plaything. These feelings hold you back slightly and therefore, for a while, you'll switch between doing a grade 0 and clean shaving. However, there comes a point where the only option is a clean shave. Grade 0 is no longer cutting the hair and it still feels too long afterwards. Yes, it's annoying and it can be frustrating at times, but you'll get used it.

38. A clean shave is now a must

Shaving Becomes a 3-4 Days a Week Task

Now that a clean shave is the only method that works, prepare for even more time in the bathroom. You'll know when it needs to be done. You can ask your friends and family for their opinion, but they may not know, as it's harder for them to notice a difference. It's up to you. The longer you wait to do it, the worse it will look, the harder it will be to shave, and the greater the time it will take. It becomes boring and tedious relatively quickly, but it will make you feel a whole lot better when you've done it.

39. Shaving becomes a 3-4 days a week task

Trying to Work Out the Best Razor or Shaver to Use

There are several products out there that can give you a good clean shave and a nice smooth head. The first few months will be trial and error. Try as many as you can afford and use them all more than once before you decide. If you have the time and money, you may find that going to a barber is the best option because they can use tools that you will need a little more practice with, like a cutthroat razor. Be patient as they will all take some getting used to in the begin.

40. Trying to work out the best razor or shaver to use

The *CONSTANT* Jokes

This is not a copy and paste error. I didn't forget that I had already mentioned it. I can count. The jokes will not go away. You may think that people will grow tired of them, but I'm afraid to say they won't. It will get very tiresome, and you'll hear the same ones over and over and over and over again. There will be some originals which you'll have to give the person credit for, but the truth is, how you deal with it is something only you can do.

41. The CONSTANT jokes

Realising How Bad It Looked

It will not take long for you to look back and reflect on years past in which you thought keeping your hair looked good. You will see for yourself that you definitely should have grabbed the clippers earlier, and that a five-finger forehead is not a good look. That, at least in my case, Mum was right, and you should've listened to her. Sorry for snapping at you those few times, Mum. The silver lining is that you are not still in that phase; you saw the light and should be thankful that it did not go on for much longer.

42. Realising how bad it looked

Looking at Others and Thinking They Need To Take the Plunge

Now this you'll have to do tastefully. There is no need to be ruthless. Whilst you are out and about, you'll undoubtedly see those who are going through the balding process. You will judge them, and you'll be thinking to yourself that they need to sort that out. Make sure you do only think it; don't say anything out loud and try not to stare. If you are with a fellow baldy, you'll probably scrutinise the person in question a little more but, again, be nice because you know it's not easy.

43. Looking at others and thinking they need to take the plunge

Trying to Offer Advice to Your Friends Who Have Finally Started the Process

If you are one of the first in your friendship group to go through this, you'll feel like you can help those in need. However, like when you were told to shave it off and didn't, your friends will most likely do the same. They will ignore you. You can try to offer advice and hint that the best option is to shave it, but they will not oblige. You can tell someone to do, or not do, something a thousand times, but until they do it themselves, they will not learn. (This is also a useful tip for life in general.)

44. Trying to offer advice to your friends who have finally started the process

Knowing It Was the Right Choice

As you continue with life, apart from the jokes as mentioned, everything will go back to as it was when you had hair. What I mean by that is: people will cease to care. You'll become comfortable with who you are. The feeling that everyone is judging and staring at you will decline. You will fade into the background. When this happens, it's easier to accept that it was the right choice.

45. Knowing it was the right choice

Wishing You Had Done It Sooner

It's easy to say this after the fact, but you will most definitely wish you'd done it sooner. I will apologise on your behalf and say sorry that you did not come to the realisation earlier. Hindsight is a wonderful thing. However, on the flip side, if you are someone who thought, "Let's just shave it now," then I am in awe and offer my most sincere congratulations. Well done.

Well done, indeed.

46. Wishing you had done it sooner

Thinking People Look Better Without Hair

Upon joining the prestigious club of baldies, you may find that you become slightly biased. What I mean by this is that, when you see someone who has shaved their head by choice but who can still grow their hair as well, you'll favour them with the shaved head. If you are watching a film and the actor or actress is bald for the part but later you see them in another film, in which they have hair, you may find yourself saying or thinking things like, "It looks so much better shorter." Or, "They should shave it again."

47. Thinking people look better without hair

The Feeling of Liberation

Although keeping the peach fuzz to a minimum and shaving more regularly adds a slight inconvenience to your life, the weight lifted off your shoulders speaks for itself. Not having to worry about how to have your hair styled or whether or not it still looks okay is liberating. Personally, despite every now and then wishing I had the ability to regrow my hair, it's not something I miss at all, and even if I could grow it, I'd still keep it shaved.

48. The feeling of liberation

Looking and Feeling Good Now You've Done It

Once you've found a routine and somewhat mastered the technique of shaving, you will gain a newfound self-confidence. Both internally and externally you'll feel good. Do not shy away and act like you have to hide this confidence in yourself from others. You should flaunt it and be proud because it's a hurdle in your life that you have overcome.

49. Looking and feeling good now you've done it

Bald is Beautiful

Being bald is nothing to be ashamed of. It doesn't change who you are, the same way that growing a beard does not change who you are. It does take some getting used to, and there will be some challenges you face along the way, these mostly being ones you manifest yourself. The overall process of receding and balding is one that can be prolonged for months, years or decades. If, like me, you can't quite accept the fact you are losing your hair early on, it will be a long journey. If, however, you're brave and just do it, then it will be a short one. It's a length of time determined by you. As I've said, people will want to touch it, they will ask questions, they will joke and they will tease, which, most of the time, will not be in spite. Think about this, if it's the only thing they joke and make fun of you for, then everything else about you must be perfect, right? Hair is not as fundamental as you think, and the sooner you realise that, the sooner you can focus on the more important things in life like your goals, your career or your love life.

Bald is not a negative thing. Bald is beautiful.

50. Bald is beautiful